Under The Lime Tree

)k!

by Nikki Emmerton

Dedication

For Issy

Foreword

This book is not simply a collection of recipes. It is a little taste of Under The Lime Tree, a magical place created by Nikki Emmerton and Sean Williams where their love of life, exuberance and enthusiasm is reflected in everything they put on the table. There is always something bubbling away on the stove, a cake in the oven filling the kitchen with delicious smells and a basket of picture perfect veggies waiting for the Nikki treatment. The vegetable garden provides Nikki with much of her inspiration and she nurtures her crops as she does her guests, with all her heart and soul. Dip into this book and you will find veggie cooking as you have never seen it before. This is food that is bursting with colour, flavour and good things, in fact very much like Nikki herself. I know you will enjoy every mouthful.

Mary Cadogan
Food writer and cookery teacher
www.marycadogan.com

simple
&
soulful
homemade
recipes from
**Under The
Lime Tree**
spa b & b
france

Pyjama Press - revised September 2015 - www.pyjamapress.com

Copyright © Nikki Emmerton

This book is sold subject to the condition that it shall not, by way of trade or otherwise, be lent, resold,

hired out, or otherwise circulated without the publisher's prior consent in any form of binding or cover

other than that in which it was published and without a similar condition including this condition

being imposed on the subsequent purchaser.

The moral right of Nikki Emmerton

to be identified as the author of this work has been asserted.

First published in the UK 2011 by Pyjama Press.

A CIP catalogue record for this book is available from the British Library.

Design by Pyjama Press, UK.

Photography and layout by Nikki Emmerton.

Printed and bound in the UK or USA by Lightning Source Ltd.

ISBN: 978-1-908000-06-4

Acknowledgements

This book would not have come about if it were not for a constant flow of friends and guests at our dinner table, asking for my recipes.

Compliments to the chef are always an enormous encouragement and a validation that their style and creativity works. That something more than a meal has taken place.

Which is exactly what happens! Something more than a meal has taken place ~ not only everyday-good food, but good food, good wine, good conversation, good fun and good company, every day! These things are, in my opinion, the great simple pleasures of life. I love caring for others and I love creating concoctions in my kitchen that will be flavour-full & filling, colourful & charismatic, simple & satisfying, nurturing & nutritious and importantly, imaginative & laced with lashings of love!

This collection of recipes from the repertoire at Under The Lime Tree is a celebration of those simple pleasures. It's a 'thank you' to everyone who has come into our lives, everyone who has spent time in our beautiful surroundings, sat at our dinner table and, albeit for a brief time, shared their love and laughter with us.

It's also a 'thank you' to my life partner & lover Sean ~ my multi-tasked & talented top-taster, chief-chopper, head-waiter and maitre'd! ~ without whom, my interest in cooking for a non-vegetarian (as he was then) would never have developed so completely, and without doubt, the magic ingredient in everything I do.

Merci à tous et Bon Appétit!

Nikki ♡

About me

It makes sense to me to eat well. In fact, it makes sense to me to live well! My desires to live well, live more off the land, and live without debt are what inspired me to leave London and a high-flying career in international business in 2000 and buy a former farm in rural France.

Being vegetarian and being in France are quite simply, incompatible! There is still no concept of what, no meat? no fish? not even occasionally? not even "un petit peu"? (a little), in the French diet. Of course, some of the larger towns or cities might be accommodating, but most of the time, you have to watch as the bacon bits are peeled off the grilled goat's cheese, or settle for salads and hope there's no tuna lurking amongst the lettuce.

The energy I put into cooking has come about because, really, there is no alternative. It's a do or die situation ~ either you cook and do it well or die of boredom from overdosing on omelettes! I chose the former. My mum was a flamboyant cook & hostess and god forbid, I have become my mother! I have inherited her kitchen know-how and have never been phased with the idea of catering.

So I opened up as a B&B to cater to those with similar dietary needs. Similar needs here meaning tasty, homemade, hearty, organic food from the garden, plenty of it too, and fairly traded where possible. Oh! and they happen to be vegetarian!

These recipes demonstrate how easy it is to provide meat free meals, no fish, not even a little bit! In fact, they show how easy it is to take a small step and leap into vegan territory with only a simple tweak here & there.

As well as cooking for Sean & my guests, I am a massage therapist. As well as being a cook and a massage therapist, I run a 30 acre site, managing the woodlands, the garden and the potager. When I am not doing any of these things, I play with my lovely bow & arrow, play with the cats, and generally, play at living as well as I can.

Recipes

Thumbs up for coconut

Derived from the Spanish cocos, meaning "monkey face" the coconut palm is so highly valued around the world, that it's known as the Tree of Life!

Nutritiously rich in vitamins & minerals, it's a valuable source of both food & medicine to over a third of the world's population. Although high in fat, over 50% of the fatty acids in coconut come from lauric acid, a known antioxidant, antiviral & antibacterial.

It is extremely beneficial in fighting off infection. (Hydrogenated coconut oil however, gets the thumbs down because all the lauric acid has been removed).

monkey madness

Virgin Coconut Oil is an excellent massage oil for Hair, Scalp & Skin

Healthy cooking
and
healthy caring

tree of life

Cauliflower & Coconut Paté
with cumin

1 Heat the oven to 200C / gas 6. Grease & line a loaf tin.

2 Cook the cauliflower florets in unsalted water, drain & cool.

3 When cool, blend with the other ingredients, adding the eggs last and seasoning with black pepper. The red onion will turn the mix slightly pink, but the contrast is worth it once cooked.

4 Pour into the prepared loaf tin and bake for about 40 minutes, or until cooked.

This is a tasty, moist and refreshing paté ~ the perfect starter to get the palette going, but substantial enough to serve as a main meal with a variety of other dishes, hot or cold or with wonderfully warmed breads

Ingredients

400g cauliflower florets

75g crème fraîche

1 red onion, roughly chopped

1 tea spoon cumin

1 dessert spoon grated coconut

200g feta cheese

50g vegetarian blue cheese

2 eggs

freshly ground black pepper

You could take the first 5 *ingredients listed above, add* a cored red apple & a pot of coconut yoghurt, then whiz in a processor with water or milk to make a delicious Summer time Soup served chilled!

anything but common

Cumin ~ a centuries old Ayurvedic medicine

It has a unique perfume, cumenaldehyde, which, together with its essential oils, exceptionally high iron content, high vitamin & mineral content makes Cumin one of nature's best over all body tonics.

It is particularly effective with all digestive disorders, providing instant relief from nausea, indigestion & acidic discomfort. Its other medicinal benefits are associated with excellent pre-natal health, **treating insomnia, regulating menstruation, boosting the immune** system, rejuvenating the skin, improving metabolism and fighting colds & respiratory ailments.

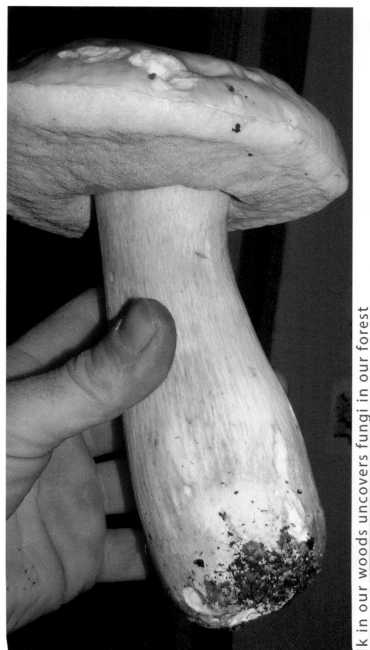

a walk in our woods uncovers fungi in our forest

Mushrooms, whether wild or cultivated are well worth the effort to add flavour, interest & nourishment.

Mushroom & Artichoke Paté
with lemon & black pepper

Mushrooms ~ a fun gi to cook with!

Ancient civilizations believed that mushrooms had super powers and modern science suggests they weren't wrong! High in minerals such as potassium, they are also a source of riboflavin, niacin & high in selenium ~ an essential trace element shown to help protect against prostate & breast cancers and heart disease.

Mushrooms are one of the top 5 natural foods for antioxidants and are the only non-animal source of vitamin D. They contain a high quantity of vitamin B12

Ingredients: serves 4

2 table spoons sesame oil

1 onion, peeled & chopped

1 heaped tea spoon ground black pepper

150 g mushrooms, wiped, destalked & finely chopped

4 artichoke hearts, drained and chopped

1 handful pitted black olives, chopped

1 cup breadcrumbs

½ lemon, juiced

1 teaspoon black olive tapenade (optional)

100g fresh parsley, chopped, reserving some for the garnish

1 Gently heat the sesame oil in a large saucepan and add the onion. Fry until translucent, then add the black pepper.

2 After two minutes tip in the chopped mushrooms and mix well. Gently heat through, then add the artichokes and olives. After a further two minutes, toss in the breadcrumbs, lemon juice and tapenade, if using.

3 Stir well, adjust the seasoning if necessary, then add the chopped fresh parsley.

Serve warm or chilled, stuffed inside a grilled Portobello mushroom, or with fresh bread, hot toast or warmed pitta

Make room for Mushrooms!

And remember, mushrooms, lemon & black pepper are a magic combination.

variations

Add a little blue cheese (but remember it's not vegan!) or a few mashed chestnuts for a protein fix, or some pine nuts for a bit of crunch.

Meet Wilma, one of our three Walnut trees

Beyond Basil

& no longer pine nuts

I simply adore pesto! I use it frequently and I'm liberal with it too. Pesto originates in Genoa, northern Italy and it comes from the Genoese word pestâ', meaning to pound or crush ~ in reference to the sauces' traditional ingredients of basil, pine nuts, grated hard cheese & olive oil. The French have a version called 'pistou' ~ generally made with basil & garlic. While cheese may be added, usually no nuts are included. The point is, that you can use any kind of green leafy veg that you have, pound it with or without nuts, with or without cheese, and pretty much add whatever you like in order to make your own version.

No one's noticing, so be novel

walnuts

Walnut Pesto
a new twist on an old favourite

Walnuts ~ food for better thought

Walnuts have long been associated with 'brain food' not only because of their 2 hemispheres & wrinkled appearance, but because of their high concentration of Omega-3 fatty acids. These are fluid & flexible structural fats found in walnuts, flaxseed and cold water fish which maximize the brain cells' ability to usher in nutrients and eliminate waste.

As well as flaxseeds, they are the best vegetarian source of Omega-3 fatty acids

1 Put all the ingredients and half the oil into a food processor and blend.

2 Drizzle in the remaining oil until you have your desired consistency.

3 Season with salt and pepper.

Serve as a dip or as a base in home made pizzas or as a topping for a pasta dish. For a more intense flavour, toast the walnuts first. For a more creamy finish, add about 50g silken tofu

Ingredients:

35 to 40g shelled walnuts, broken

2 garlic cloves, peeled

1 tea spoon lemon juice

100ml olive oil

50g or more of any green leafy stuff: for instance ~ fresh basil, spinach, parsley, watercress and some frozen peas for luck

salt & pepper to taste

magical melatonin

Walnuts contain melatonin in a bio-available form (which means we can absorb it). Melatonin is a powerful antioxidant and a hormone produced by the pineal gland, which is involved in inducing and regulating sleep.

So for a better brain and a better night's sleep, serve walnuts at night.

B for Broccoli and B for Bravo

Broccoli is part of the cruciferous family of vegetables (named after the cross shape of their 4-petalled flowers) which are among the best all-round nutrition boosters. It's a rich source of the vitamin B complex (particularly B2, B3 & B6), as well as vitamins C & A and K. It has a very high mineral content of iron, folic acid, fibre, potassium & calcium ~ even more than a glass of milk.

But the real benefit of broccoli is as an anti cancer food

The presence of vital antioxidants have demonstrated tremendous anti cancer effects, particularly for breast cancer.

Broccoli & Green Pea Soup
with pesto

Steam or stir fry broccoli to keep its goodness in

1 Melt the margarine in a large pan and add the onion. Fry gently for 5 minutes, then add the chilli pepper, soy sauce and apple.

2 After 2 minutes stir in the pesto. Add the broccoli stalks first of all and continue frying for 1 minute. Toss in the florets and mix well into the other ingredients.

3 Add the frozen peas and enough water to cover all the veg. Slowly simmer with the lid on for 10 minutes.

4 Take off the heat and allow to cool. Blend in a food processor until the desired consistency ~ adding a little more water if need be. (Don't overdo it though! You can always thin a soup but you can't make it thicker.)

5 Heat through gently when ready to serve, seasoning with salt & pepper to taste and swirling with yoghurt.

Serve with warmed walnut bread

Ingredients: serves 2

40g margarine

1 onion, peeled & chopped

1 red chilli pepper, deseeded & chopped

1 tea spoon soy sauce

1 apple, cored & chopped

1 dessert spoon pesto

1 broccoli, florets & some of the stalk, chopped

200g frozen peas

water to cover

salt & pepper

1 small pot soy yoghurt

Swirl
a spiral
of soy
yoghurt
into your
soup

Ingredients: serves 4

2 knobs of vegan margarine

1 red onion, chopped

2 garlic cloves, peeled & chopped

1 tea spoon fresh ginger, grated

1 apple, cored & chopped

400gms cooked beetroot, roughly chopped

100ml orange juice

water to cover

a twist of fresh black pepper

a handful of chives, chopped

swirl of soy yoghurt to garnish

Borscht is not from Russia after all. The Ukraine lays claim to it. The word derives from "br'sch" in old Slavic language, which means beet, but some recipes don't even require beetroot at all

Beautiful Borscht
beautiful beetroot

If, like me, you were forced to have manky old beetroot at school, then it's easy to be put off for life. Which is a shame. It's versatile, very useful & very easy to add to any dish or diet

1 Melt the margarine in a large saucepan and add the onion.

2 Fry gently for 2 minutes then add the garlic, ginger and apple.

3 Crack in lots of black pepper and mix well. Add the beetroot and stir in. Continue to cook gently for a further 5 minutes. Add the orange juice and water ~ just enough to cover the vegetables then simmer for 10 minutes.

4 Allow to cool, then process in a blender.

5 Reheat when ready to serve

Serve with chopped chives sprinkled on top and a final crack of black pepper. Place a swirl of soy yoghurt on top

fritillaria meleagris

borage officinalis

Salad of Baked Beetroot
with mango chutney

Both the leaves and the root are nutritious and have many medicinal properties. The root is rich in folic acid, potassium, manganese, fibre, boron & beta-carotene, while the leaves are a rich source of iron, calcium, and vitamins C & A. The presence of iron, folate & magnesium help in blood production, making it a valuable food for those suffering from anaemia

1 In a large bowl, mix the beetroot with a table spoon or two of the mango chutney. Taste and test!

2 Don't add too much chutney ~ you're looking to enhance the natural sweetness & flavour of the beetroot, not turn it into chutney with a bit of beet added! It will soften and mash up as you mix in the mango, so take care here too.

3 When you're satisfied, serve heaped into a pile with tomato wedges decorated around the beetroot for a very simple but impressive effect.

4 Sprinkle some chopped coriander or parsley or basil on top, crack a little black pepper and sea salt over the lot and serve.

Ingredients: serves 8

500g cooked beetroot, broken into pieces or grated (pat dry with kitchen paper if necessary)

2 to 3 table spoons of sweet mango chutney

4 to 5 large tomatoes, cut into wedges

salt & pepper to taste

chopped coriander or parsley or basil to garnish

Great as a side salad or a condiment to a main meal. It's very refreshing & a colourful delight to add to any table

variations

Beetroot... go raw & grate it into salads; dice or slice & season with balsamic; char-grill with a dash of olive oil; peel like potato & deep fry; better still, bake into a brownie.

Try adding some slices of real mango as an alternative to the tomatoes. They're packed with antioxidants, vitamins and minerals.

If you can get hold of beetroot leaves and not just the root, use them up in a salad. Treat them just like spinach. They're very good for you and gorgeous too.

Ras el Hanout

a popular blend of spices from North Africa

The name means 'top of the shop' in Arabic and refers to the best mixes a seller has to offer. Although there is no set combination of spices, typically it would contain

cardamom, coriander, turmeric, cumin, clove, nutmeg, ground chilli pepper, fenugreek, fennel and garlic to name but a few.

There can be up to 50 spices included in the best mixes, all of which are toasted before being ground up together.

The overall effect is an extremely versatile ingredient greater than its individual components ~ adding a golden colour and aromatic, curry-like floral flavours & subtle nuances to a tagine, couscous, rice, tofu or aubergine dish.

Transcend the ordinary by adding it to your cooking today

Nik's no Need to Knead Bread

1 Heat the oven to 180C / gas 4.

2 In a large bowl, mix all the ingredients in order, only adding the nuts and fruit when the rest of the ingredients have been mixed thoroughly. It's quite a wet mixture.

3 Divide the mixture between 2 greased 1kg loaf tins (they should be half full) and allow to rise for about 1 hour at around 50C. (You can set the oven at this temperature first if the ambient temperature is too cold). It doesn't double in size, which is normal.

4 Bake at 180C for 1 to 1 1/2 hours.

Eat with relish, old bean

Ingredients

300g spelt flour

200g plain flour

2 tea spoons salt

1 dessert spoon raspberry vinegar

1 dessert spoon honey

1 packet dried yeast

1 dessert spoon 'Ras el Hanout' spice mix

500ml tonic or sparkling water

250g mixed nuts, roughly chopped (eg. walnuts, hazelnuts, linseeds etc)

200g mixed dried fruit, chopped (eg. golden raisins, apricots, dates etc)

the aroma of fresh bread

Some things in life can't be beaten ~ one of them is the aroma of freshly baked delicious bread ...

... others are a good stretch with the rising sun (Toby does it on my behalf while I'm still sipping coffee), a good scrub, and last but not least, a much needed cat nap after catching up on the news.

17

harvesting our own produce at UTLT is simply SO satisfying

Suggestions

Why not use whatever's ready in the garden ~ sweat peas, mange tout, beetroot, red & green cabbage, broccoli, carrots, spinach, swiss chard ~ or even green olives & capers

Ingredients: serves 2

- 3 to 4 table spoons olive oil
- 1 large onion, peeled & chopped
- 1 red chilli, deseeded & finely chopped
- ¼ aubergine, roughly chopped
- ¼ fennel bulb, sliced
- ½ courgette, sliced into rounds
- ¼ red pepper, chopped
- 2 tomatoes, cut into wedges
- 100g french beans, cooked
- handful finely sliced red cabbage (optional)
- 400ml jar of good quality tomato sauce
- 1 dessert spoon blackcurrant jam
- handful fresh thyme
- handful fresh parsley or basil
- 100g soft rind goat's cheese

Ratatouille
with Goat's Cheese

1 On a moderately high setting, heat the oil in a large sauce pan, then add the onion. Let it cook for a couple of minutes then toss in the chopped chilli and aubergine. Sprinkle over the fresh thyme and stir well to coat all the veg.

2 After 5 minutes add the fennel, courgette, pepper, tomato wedges, red cabbage (if using), french beans and stir in.

3 Allow to cook for 2 mins, then add the tomato sauce, blackcurrant jam and follow immediately with the fresh parsley or basil.

4 Cover and cook for a further 5 mins. turning down the heat.

5 About 3 minutes from the end of cooking, grease a baking tray with oil and set the grill to high. Place the cut slices of goat's cheese on the oiled baking tray and grill until lightly browned and softened.

Pile the ratatouille onto a plate and serve with a slice of grilled goat's cheese in the middle

What is ratatouille?

It's a classic vegetable dish from the Provence region of France. The first half of its name is believed to be slang for "chunky stew", while the second half is from the french touillir - to stir. It can be stewed or sautéed, as here, and is either a side dish or main course served with couscous, rice or potatoes.

vegan variation

To make it Vegan

Of course, forget the goat's cheese if you want to make this dish Vegan.

Ingredients: serves 4

Pre-prep

1 aubergine, thinly sliced in rounds, then halved

2 table spoons turmeric

1 tea spoon sea salt

1-2 table spoons sunflower oil, per batch of frying

Preparation

3 table spoons sunflower oil

1 table spoon fenugreek seeds

1 large onion, peeled & chopped

1 tea spoon madras curry powder

1 tea spoon garam masala

1 dessert spoon lime pickle

2 large tomatoes, cut into wedges

400g jar of cooked chickpeas

200ml coconut milk

6 large fresh spinach leaves, torn

the active ingredient in turmeric is curcumin

Aubergine & Chickpea Curry
with turmeric

Turmeric is one of Nature's most powerful healers. It's an anti-inflammatory, antiseptic, antibacterial, and antioxidant. It's a liver detoxifier, and a pain killer. It's used in the treatment of depression, Alzheimer's, certain cancers, digestive disorders & helps metabolise fat.

1 Pre-prep: Mix the turmeric with the salt in a bowl, then coat each slice of aubergine with it. Heat the oil in a large frying pan, and when hot, drop in the aubergine slices and fry on both sides. Set aside. Continue frying all the aubergine in this way, using more oil as necessary. Allow to cool.

2 For the rest, gently heat the oil in a large saucepan. Add the fenugreek seeds and after 2 mins, add the chopped onions and stir well. When they are translucent, sprinkle in the curry powder & garam masala and keep stirring. Add the lime pickle and mix well. Allow to gently bubble for a minute then add the tomatoes, the chickpeas, the coconut milk, the prepared aubergines and finally, the torn spinach leaves.

3 Simmer very gently with the lid on for 10 to 15 minutes, stirring occasionally, until ready to serve.

Serve with rice, Indian flat breads & side dishes and chutneys & pickles

Turmeric

2,500 years ago, it's original use was as a natural yellow dye ~ if you don't wear gloves in the pre-prep stage, you'll look like you've been smoking 40 a day.

wear gloves

Pan Fried Chestnuts With Quinoa
caramelised onions and sun dried tomatoes

Cultivated for more than 2000 years in the Andean mountains of Peru, quinoa (pronounced keenwa) is the sacred grain of the Incas. Reputed for its exceptional nutritional qualities, it is rich in protein, fibres, minerals, most notably phosphorus, magnesium, iron and is equally rich in vitamins E, B1, and B6. Is it any wonder it was considered sacred?

1 Heat the sesame & sun dried tomato oil in a large saucepan. Add a twist or two of black pepper, then tip in the brown sugar. Stir well and when dissolved, add the sliced onions and gently fry. Put the lid on and allow to sweat on a low heat for about 20 to 25 mins. Check on them from time to time ~ they don't want to be too mushy.

2 After 10 minutes begin to cook the quinoa according to packet instructions. It will take about 15 minutes.

3 After 20 minutes of caramelising the onions, add the chestnuts, the sun dried tomatoes, thyme and rocket for the last 5 minutes of cooking (if the quinoa is not ready at the same time, turn the heat off the onions and keep covered until it is). Like rice, quinoa should have absorbed all the water when cooked.

Serve it with the chestnut mix heaped on top

Ingredients: serves 4

2 table spoons sesame oil for frying

3 table spoons oil from the sun dried tomatoes

freshly ground black pepper

2 table spoons brown sugar

4 onions, peeled & sliced

2 cups of Quinoa

fresh or dried thyme

500g jar of cooked whole chestnuts, some halved

285g sun dried tomatoes, chopped

handful of rocket

wild about nuts

Nothing reminds me more of cold, wintery London nights than the aroma of roasted chestnuts wafting in on a chilly wind. Wrapped in cones by street sellers stamping their feet to keep warm, we lingered in front of their burning braziers, savouring the smokey earthliness and burning our tongues on hot, blackened skins. Painfully delicious. At the end of the year, chestnuts are a great wild food to forage and roast at home. Rich both in (complex) carbs & proteins but low in calories & cholesterol they've earned the nickname "L'Arbre de Pain" here in France, literally, the tree of bread.

Add in or substitute with ~
sun dried tomatoes
peanuts
buffalo mozzarella
sweet corn
red kidney beans
~ just keep the colour scheme
going

S l o w   f o o d

to keep you going

Red lentils, apricots & almonds are rich in a wide range of nutrients, high in fibre but slow to digest ~ stabilizing blood sugar & insulin levels after a meal, providing a steady flow of energy.

Generally, all pulses are a good source of protein, calcium, B vitamins & potassium

22

Red Lentil Bake
with apricots & almonds

Almonds are where it's at

Almonds have a reputation as a superfood and are considered one of the healthiest nuts to eat. Rich in the right fats ~ heart healthy monounsaturated fats ~ they help to raise 'good' HDL & lower 'bad' LDL cholesterol levels. They're high in potassium & low in sodium which helps to regulate blood pressure and their high fibre content acts to detoxify the body

Ingredients: serves 4

250g red lentils

1 large potato, or sweet potato, washed, sliced & part boiled

oil for frying

1 medium (red) onion, chopped

1 table spoon grated fresh ginger

1 handful dried apricots, chopped

1 heaped tea spoon harissa (chilli sauce)

2 handfuls flaked almonds

sprinkle of cayenne pepper

1 Cook the red lentils according to packet instructions. When cooked, drain (if necessary) then set aside.

2 In a separate pan, part boil the potato or sweet potato in a little salted water, drain & set aside.

3 Heat the oven to 180 oC / gas 4. Whilst the lentils and potato are cooking, fry the onion & ginger in a little oil in a large saucepan and stir well.

4 After a further 5 minutes, stir in the apricots & harissa then turn off the heat. Combine well with the red lentil mixture.

5 Layer the potato into an oven proof dish. Spoon the lentil mix on top, smooth it out a little with a fork, sprinkle over the almonds and cayenne pepper.

6 Pop in the oven and bake until golden brown. The ingredients are already cooked, so you're just looking to bind everything together in the oven. About 15 minutes.

Serve with a lovely garden salad or char-grilled veg ... or with a little of whatever you fancy

Tahini

~ tiny but tough

Tahini is a tasty paste of lightly roasted sesame seeds widely used throughout the Middle East and a key ingredient in falafels and houmous. If you can't get hold of it, sesame paste or butter is the perfect alternative. Sesame seeds are high in minerals, fibre and antioxidants. Add them as a sprinkle to many dishes ~ from salads to soups, potatoes to porridge.

Falafels

100g breadcrumbs

300g cooked chickpeas, drained

1 onion, roughly chopped

1 heaped tea spoon cumin

1 tea spoon coriander

1 tea spoon salt

1 tea spoon baking powder

1 table spoon tahini

1 table spoon lemon juice

small handful of parsley

1 Combine all the ingredients in a food processor until well mixed, or by hand in a large bowl. It's quite a dry mix. Chill for 30 minutes at least.

2 Remove from the fridge and make into small rounds or ovals with your hands, adding a little water if necessary, then flatten slightly ~ makes about 16.

3 Place on a lined baking tray in a medium to hot oven turning frequently until golden brown.

Mezze ~ from the old Persian word "maza" meaning taste or relish

24

Middle Eastern Mezze
with falafels, salads & houmous

Aubergine & Courgette Salad

1 aubergine, sliced into thin rounds

1 courgette

2 table spoons olive oil

juice of one orange

small handful each of

fresh mint & coriander

ground black pepper

1 Brush both sides of the aubergine lightly with a little of the olive oil and place on a baking tray. Cook under a pre-heated grill or on a griddle for 3 minutes on both sides until lightly browned. Set aside to cool.

2 Using a vegetable peeler, slice the courgette into ribbons.

3 Place the rest of the oil and all the ingredients in a bowl and toss with the aubergine & courgette.

Tabouleh

2 cups of quinoa

1 roasted red pepper from a jar

¼ cucumber

handful fresh mint

handful fresh coriander

juice of ½ lemon

1 Cook the quinoa in 2 1/2 cups of salted water. Allow to cool completely.

2 When cool, chop and toss all the other ingredients in a serving bowl to combine with the lemon juice.

Houmous

300g cooked chickpeas, drained

5 table spoons olive oil

1 heaped tea spoon cumin

1 tea spoon salt

1 dessert spoon tahini

juice of ½ lemon

1 Combine all the ingredients in a blender until the desired consistency, drizzling in more oil for a smoother finish.

Tofu takes a tumble
in the tabloids

Tofu gets a lot of bad press, which is shame, because it's a very worthy ingredient. It's packed full of nutrients and is the richest non-dairy source of calcium. It's high in iron & potassium & contains omega-3 fatty acids which may help to lower blood cholesterol. Tofu may also ease menopausal systems since it has lots of weak oestrogen-like compounds. Evidence suggests that it has some anti-breast cancer activity for the same reason. Always have the right kind of tofu for your recipe ~ firm or silken. Firm tofu can be cubed, crumbled, sliced or smoked. It can be marinated, sautéed, scrambled, kebabed or grilled. Pat it dry and do what you like! Silken tofu is much softer so it is often used blended with other ingredients to make dressings or cakes. And it's widely available without being genetically modified. Check it out.

From garden plot ...

Caramelised Onion & Spiced Tofu Tart
with goat's cheese & sun dried tomatoes

1 Part boil the potatoes (about 5 minutes) then drain & set aside to cool. On a flat surface, pat the tofu dry with kitchen towel then crumble roughly with a fork. Tip into a bowl and toss with the chilli sauce. Allow to marinade while the potatoes are cooking.

2 Melt the butter in a large saucepan, add the sliced onions and season well with S & P. Gently fry with the lid on for 5 mins. When they are soft and transparent, add the sugar & stir. Simmer gently with the lid on for 10 minutes.

3 Heat the oven to 180C / gas 4.

4 Roll out the pastry into a greased flan dish. Line the pastry first with the sliced potatoes, then tip in the tofu mix. Spoon the onion mix on top of the tofu. Arrange the sliced goat's cheese on top (if using) covering the whole of the tart, then randomly sprinkle over the sun dried tomatoes.

5 Bake for about 30 minutes, or until the pastry is cooked.

Leave to cool to allow the tart to set but serve warm

Ingredients: serves 6

250g potato, peeled, sliced & part boiled

400g firm tofu, drained & crumbled with a fork

1 table spoon harissa or other chilli sauce

50g butter

5 large onions, peeled & sliced

2 table spoons brown sugar

1 packet ready made pastry (or make your own)

200g goat's cheese, sliced

8 sun dried tomatoes, chopped

salt & pepper

vegan variation

To make it Vegan

Omit the goat's cheese & use margarine instead of butter. Use honey or maple syrup instead of all the sugar, but bear in mind vegans don't eat honey.

27

Globe Artichocke

Aids digestion & assists liver function. Steam or boil fresh globe heads for 30 to 40 mins. Pick off one leaf at a time, dip in a piquant sauce & drag the flesh off with your teeth. Very primitive & great fun. Also makes a fab centrepiece table decoration..

sooo good salad

28

Apples

Packed with health boosting properties. Most of the goodness is in the skin however, so wash well & keep it on! Add one to your soups for undetectable delectable goodness.

Ingredients: serves 4

Salad

400g cooked chickpeas, drained

240g artichoke hearts, drained & halved

125g organic sweet corn, drained

1 medium red apple, cored & sliced

2 cups shelled walnuts, toasted

Dressing

1 heaped dessert spoon Dijon mustard

3 heaped dessert spoons mayonnaise

2 cloves garlic, crushed

½ lemon juice

black pepper

Artichoke, Apple & Chickpea Salad
with toasted walnuts

1 Drain all the Salad Ingredients.

2 Char-grill the artichokes then allow to cool.

3 Gently toast the walnuts and allow to cool.

4 In a small bowl mix together all the Dressing Ingredients.

5 In a large serving bowl, mix the chickpeas & corn together with the dressing ~ adding a little at a time so as not to overdo it. Toss in the apple, then finally add the artichokes and sprinkle the walnuts on top.

This is quite a filling salad, so serve it as a main course for 4, or as a starter for 6

Chick peas

Contain high levels of protein & are easily digestible. They're a very good source of folate, manganese & copper, and low in sodium & saturated fat. Get chic with chickpeas and include them in your diet.

Sweet corn

Provides more starch and calories than most vegetables. A good food for steady blood sugar levels. Scrumptiously sensational straight from the cob.

vegan variation

To make a Vegan dressing

In a food processor, blend until smooth and creamy:

300g silken tofu

1 tea spoon Dijon mustard

½ tea spoon salt

1 table spoon sugar

2 table spoons apple cider vinegar

29

Pickled nasturtiums

Capers are pricey. Pickled nasturtium seeds are an inexpensive substitute. Try this recipe to make your own

fill a ¹litre jar (or ⁴small ones) with nasturtium seeds

¹litre apple cider vinegar

²teaspoons pickling salt

¹medium onion· thinly sliced

½lemon· thinly sliced

¹teaspoon pickling spice

¹clove garlic· smashed

⁴to ⁶peppercorns

½teaspoon celery seed

Preparation

1 Pick the seeds when they are still green.

2 Combine all the other ingredients in a large saucepan & bring to the boil.

3 Simmer for 5 minutes, remove from the heat & allow to cool.

4 Pour cooled mixture over the seeds and refrigerate for 1 week before using.

Capers are un-ripened buds from a small bush native to the Middle East & Mediterranean regions. Fresh blossoms are sun dried then pickled in brine to bring out their tangy lemony flavour. Yum yum. Nasturtiums are prolific in our garden & their young leaves are delicious in salads.

An interesting thing about paella, is that traditionally, the rice is short grain & cooked with the main dish, much like an Italian risotto. You can try this too, but I don't cook it this way since it makes the veg too soft & mushy.

Spanish Paella
with pesto

Paella ~ almost any summer veg can be used

Use frozen peas instead of french beans, throw in a couple of sliced roasted red peppers, add some pine nuts, use chopped spinach instead of rocket ~ but one of the key things to keep is capers

1 Cook the rice according to packet instructions. (I tend to bring it to the boil, then switch off the heat. The water's hot enough still to simmer the rice in the appropriate amount of water, without it all being lost to steam). Stir in the tea spoon of turmeric which of course, will colour it yellow.

2 Gently heat about 3 table spoons of olive oil in a large frying pan, preferably a paella dish if you have one. Season with lashings of ground black pepper then toss in the onion. Sauté for 5 minutes, then add the tofu. Stir frequently to brown the onion and tofu on all sides.

3 If using fresh asparagus, blanch the spears and keep them whole, adding them to the dish at the last minute. Otherwise, use a preserved version, drain, chop and add them at this stage, along with all the other ingredients, except the rocket and lemon. Stir well to incorporate all the veg and the flavours.

4 Cook gently for a further 5 minutes, then add the rocket, the lemon juice (and the fresh asparagus) ~ turn off the heat.

5 Push all the ingredients to one side of the pan, tip in the cooked rice then fold into the veg.

Add vegetarian hard cheese shavings if you don't need this recipe to be vegan. Serve in the paella dish decorated with the lemon wedges ~ et voila ... buena appetite

Vegan

Ingredients: serves 4

olive oil for cooking

1 red onion, peeled, quartered & chopped

200g tofu, cubed

5 asparagus spears, fresh if available

4 artichoke hearts, drained & sliced

6 pieces sun dried tomatoes, chopped

1 table spoon pesto

2 table spoons capers

100g french beans

100g sweet corn, drained

handful of rocket

juice of half a lemon & lemon wedges to serve

rice for 4 people

1 tea spoon turmeric (saffron is the traditional flavouring, but it's expensive & less good for you)

Sour Cream

4 dessert spoons mayonnaise

1 dessert spoon crème fraîche

3 cloves garlic

salt & pepper

1 Mix the mayonnaise and crème fraîche together in a small bowl. Peel and press the garlic into it, combine well, season with salt & pepper and leave to stand before serving.

Tomato Salsa

4 large tomatoes, roughly chopped & drained

1 dessert spoon harissa chilli sauce

2 handfuls fresh parsley, finely chopped

1 Put the chopped tomatoes in a colander and place a weight on top to drain all the liquid out. This step keeps the salsa from being watery & is worth the extra effort. Combine all ingredients in a mixing bowl. You can make the salsa as hot as you like of course, so add the harissa cautiously and to taste.

Chillies

~ king of spices

The key chemical component is Capsaicin and its mostly in the seeds & fleshy white membrane. *Mais attention!* Be careful how you handle fresh chillies ~ they can burn & irritate badly.

All varieties of chillies, even dried and powdered versions, are packed with nutrients & minerals and are known to act as a natural pain killer, reduce joint inflammation, lower blood sugar levels, inhibit prostate cancer cell growth, prevent stomach ulcers and as we all know, relieve congestion.

So, for clear sinuses, slice this spice into your supper soon

Mexican Veg Chilli
with guacamole, salsa & sour cream

Veg Chilli

2 cups green lentils
1 onion, peeled & chopped
1 carrot, grated
1 packet fajita spice mix [1]
125g red kidney beans, cooked
125g sweet corn, drained
400ml jar of good quality tomato sauce
handful fresh parsley, chopped
olive oil for frying
1 packet tortillas
100g strong grated vegetarian cheese for serving

1 Cook the lentils according to instructions, drain if necessary and set aside.

2 While the lentils are cooking, heat the oil in a large frying pan. Toss in the chopped onions and sauté for 5 minutes. Stir in the grated carrot & fajita spice mix [1]. The key to a good mexican flavour is smoked chilli ~ check it's in the mix. After 2 minutes, add the tomato sauce, & stir in the kidney beans & sweet corn.

3 Cover and simmer on a very low heat. When the lentils are cooked, add to the onion mix, with the fresh parsley. Transfer to a serving dish and keep warm.

4 Place the tortillas under a warm grill for a minute.

Guacamole

2 ripe avocados
1 finely chopped onion
juice of 1 lemon
sea salt

1 Scoop the avocado flesh into a bowl. Toss in the finely chopped onion. Season well with sea salt. Beat together with a fork, adding the lemon juice in stages until the desired taste. The juice will prevent the avocado from discolouring and add a tangy flavour but don't overdo it.

Serves 4 *Serve all dishes separately with the veg chilli as the centre piece. It's a real DIY dinner, where everyone rolls their own*

33

More Peas Please!

Did you know ...

...that Peas contain many of the B group vitamins and are the *richest* food source of vitamin B1 ~ also known as Thiamin ~ essential for normal heart, muscle & nerve cell function.

They are power packed with loads of other vitamins such as C, A and K and folate. They are an excellent source of iron, and have considerable amounts of zinc, manganese, calcium, potassium and magnesium.

They contain as much protein & energy as meat and are one of the best sources of soluble fibre.

Scrumptious Sweet & Sour Stir Fry
with green peas & cucumber

This stir fry is an eclectic mix of subtle flavours and textures to tantalize the taste buds! Hot ginger is contrasted with cool cucumber and refreshing lemon. Soft tofu is contrasted with crunchy cashew while the coconut and coriander bring it all together to create an easy Thai style dinner!

1 Put all the ingredients for the marinade in a bowl and leave to stand for a couple of hours.

2 Heat the oil in a large saucepan then add the tofu marinade, onion and chilli.

3 Fry for 5 minutes over a moderate heat.

4 Add the fennel and after 2 minutes the cabbage, cooked broccoli and cashews. Continue frying for 2 minutes.

5 Add the frozen peas and cucumber slices. Pour in the coconut milk & coriander and stir well to heat through, stirring occasionally.

Serve with noodles

Vegan

Ingredients: serves 4

Pre-prep ~ Marinade

250g firm tofu cubed

½ lemon squeezed

1 dessert spoon freshly grated ginger

3 table spoons sweet & sour sauce

Main

3 table spoons sesame oil

1 onion peeled & chopped

2 chilli peppers de-seeded & chopped

¼ fresh fennel sliced

100g green cabbage shredded

100g broccoli florets cooked

50g cashew nuts

100g frozen peas

½ cucumber sliced into half moons

200ml coconut milk

50g fresh coriander

variations

Frozen peas retain a high level of their nutrients, making peas one of the most popular and versatile foods.

Try using any green veg seasonally available ~ spinach, french beans, curly kale or even cauliflower florets ~

35

power to our pumpkins

Roasted Pumpkin
with feta cheese & black olives

1 Heat the oven to 190C / gas 5. Pour a little olive oil into a roasting dish and crack black pepper into it. Toss in the cubed pumpkin, mix the oil in with your hands ~ go on, they'll love the treat ~ then pop in the oven until just tender, 20 to 25 minutes.

2 After 10 minutes put the pasta on to boil. (A dash of oil in the water helps to keep the pasta separate).

3 10 minutes from the end of roasting the pumpkin, put the walnuts into a baking tray and pop them in the oven too.

4 5 minutes from the end of roasting, put the feta & olives into a separate tray, and pop them in just to warm through.

5 Drain the pasta and tip into a serving bowl. Take out the pumpkin, walnuts and feta.

6 Tip the pumpkin over the pasta, followed by the feta cheese & olives.

Scatter over the roasted walnuts

Ingredients: serves 2

olive oil for roasting

lashings of black pepper!

700g pumpkin, uncooked weight, peeled* & cubed

Penne pasta for 2

2 handfuls shelled & broken walnuts, roasted

200g feta cheese, patted dry & cubed

2 handfuls pitted black olives, halved

Peel the pumpkin only if it's really tough ~ the skin is the source of their health benefits

The natural sweetness of the pumpkin balances beautifully with the saltiness of the feta, so don't be tempted to change the cheese.

The walnuts are from our own garden which makes them inexpensive all year round, but you could use flaked almonds instead. Penne pasta works well in this recipe ~ other types would be equally delicious.

variations

Carotenes are the pigments that give most of the orange, red and yellow colour to vegetables and fruit. The more intense the colour, the higher the content of anti oxidants, and the better they are for you.

Leafy dark green vegetables are also high in carotenes but the colour is masked by green chlorophyll.

37

Perfect Pizzas

Basic ingredients:

pizza dough (bought or home made) and 1 dessert spoon vegetarian pesto (bought or home made). Roll out the dough into a greased 30cm pizza tin then spread the pesto over. The pesto adds loads of subtle but noticeable flavour. Have your toppings ready as soon as you're ready to roll...

To the pesto base, add your toppings in layers. A layer of grated cheese helps to seal all the flavours in, but is optional.

Other toppings could be ~ asparagus, grilled aubergine, grated courgette, mushrooms, leeks, Mozzarella, blue or goat's cheeses. You can scatter or place the ingredients as your mood suits you.

Pre heat the oven to 230C / gas 8. Bake for 15 to 20 minutes, or until the top is browned & the base crisp.

Black olive

grated hard cheese

pitted black olives cut in half

chopped sun dried tomatoes

capers

salt & pepper

Cherry tomato

grated hard cheese

thinly sliced cooked potato

2 sliced tomatoes

½ courgette grated and patted dry

2 table spoons good quality tomato sauce

cherry tomatoes cut in half

green olives cut in half

sun dried tomatoes sliced

dried herbs

salt & pepper

Broccoli & artichoke

grated hard cheese

1 onion, peeled & chopped

4 chopped artichoke hearts

chopped broccoli florets

1 chopped red pepper

capers

sprinkle of dried thyme

garnish with fresh rocket

salt & pepper

Lemon Crunch
on a ginger biscuit base

Ingredients

For the base

75g butter, melted

200g ginger biscuits, finely crushed

For the topping

100g brown sugar

100g rolled oats

75g soft margarine (chilled)

50g sesame seeds

For the filling

400ml lemon curd

1 For the base: grease & line a cake tin about 15cm in diameter. Mix the melted butter with the crushed ginger biscuits, press into the cake tin to cover the base evenly then chill in the fridge for 20 minutes.

2 For the topping: in a large bowl, mix all the ingredients until they look like fine breadcrumbs (makes a great crumble topping).

3 Heat the oven to 180C /gas 4. Remove the base from the fridge and spread with the lemon curd. Tip the topping over, press down firmly with the back of a spoon.

4 Bake for 25 to 30 minutes, or until golden on top.

Serve with cream or crème fraîche

Home Made Lemon Curd

180g melted butter

190g brown &/or white sugar

4 free range eggs

2 free range egg yolks

150ml lemon juice (5 or 6 lemons)

zest of 1 lemon

1 Gently melt the butter in a heavy based pan. Mix the butter & sugar together and beat with an electric mixer for 1 minute. Beat the eggs together, then slowly add to the sugar mix. Beat for 1 min, then whilst still beating, slowly add the lemon juice & zest.

2 Cook over a medium heat, stirring constantly with a wooden spoon until the mixture thickens - about 7 to 10 minutes. It should leave a path on the back of the spoon. Don't let it boil.

3 Transfer to sterilized jars before it cools (it continues to thicken as it cools).

Makes about 475ml

The little lemon is a wonder warrior against cardiac, digestive, dental, & diabetic problems and is a means of boosting tissue regeneration & immunity. It's a natural anti histamine, anti viral and the juice is an excellent cleanser & detoxifier.

Did you know ...

The banana is actually a giant herb, in the same family as lilies, orchids & palms. It's the largest plant on earth without a woody stem and is the most popular fruit in the world. It's possibly also the oldest, with archaeological digs revealing its cultivation as early as 8000 BC.

Nik's Red Hot Nana's
with a secret ingredient

1 Peel & slice the bananas into a bowl then squeeze the lemon juice over to prevent them from discolouring while you make the sauce.

2 Drop the knob of butter into a pan and gently heat through. Add either the caramel sauce or maple syrup, then the brown sugar and stir well. You may need a dash of water if the sauce appears too thick.

3 Add the sliced bananas and mix in without breaking up the bananas if possible.

4 Sprinkle with hot chilli pepper ~ sparingly! ~ stir in, then serve immediately.

Serve hot with vanilla ice cream

Ingredients: serves 4

4 ripe bananas

½ lemon juice

knob of butter

1 dessert spoon caramel sauce

or 1 dessert spoon maple syrup

1 table spoon raw cane sugar

a dash of water, if necessary

gentle sprinkle of hot chilli pepper ~ the secret ingredient

Ripe bananas are best for this recipe ~ so it's a great way of using up those blackening torpedoes on the edge of the fruit bowl

going bananas

It's biggest ingredient is potassium, essential for the heart, nervous system, kidneys, bones & muscles. It's natural sugars content make it a great 'pick up' and vitamins C & B6 are in abundance.

41

Food of the Gods?

Chemical compounds in the cocoa bean cause the release of certain 'happy' neuro-transmitters known to increase the level of endorphins & other opiates in the brain. They help to lessen the experience of pain, stress and depression. One such compound is Anandamide ~ ananda, a Sanskrit word for Bliss ~ which closely resembles TCH (tetrahydrocannabinol) a chemical found in marijuana. Both activate the production of dopamine, which leads to a feeling of wellbeing associated with a high.

Recipe for romance?

Another compound released by chocolate is Phenylethylamine. This "chocolate amphetamine" works like amphetamines to increase mood & decrease depression (but doesn't result in the same addiction). Phenylethylamine is also called the "love drug" because it causes changes in blood pressure & blood sugar levels leading to feelings of excitement & alertness, and causes the pulse rate to quicken, resulting in a similar feeling to when we are in love.

Chocolate
~ the chocoholic truth

It has a long history associated with feelings of wellbeing ~ it can lift your mood and lower stress & depression ~ it's considered a comfort food amongst women ~ it's the number one gift as an aperitif for Love ~ but what is it?.

Not all chocolate is made equal. The health benefits of chocolate are all locked up in the cocoa content. Of all foods, the cocoa bean has the highest levels of antioxidants ~ ever. These compounds are called flavanols, but they're very bitter. So in many cases, the flavanols have been taken out to make the chocolate taste better. So the higher the cocoa content, the greater the health benefit.

Chocolate Mousse
in minutes

1 Grease 6 ramekins or 6 shot glasses for serving.

2 Break up the chocolate into a heat-proof bowl. Place over a pan of steaming water, making sure the bowl fits tightly over the pan. Stir until smooth with a wooden spatula. Remove from the heat when melted, but don't let the chocolate cool too much.

3 Beat the sugar & egg yolks until pale & thick, then fold into the melted chocolate with a metal spoon. Add the crème fraîche & orange juice.

4 Whisk the egg whites and when firm, lightly fold into the chocolate mixture. Pour into the prepared ramekins or shot glasses and chill for at least 3 hours.

5 Bring to room temperature before serving.

Very rich and temptingly tantalising

Ingredients: serves 6

200g 70% dark chocolate

100g 70% dark chocolate with orange zest pieces

3 eggs, separated

50ml crème fraîche

50g caster sugar

1 dessert spoon orange juice

To the melting chocolate you could add ~ 1 tablespoon of your favourite spirit, 1 tablespoon of vanilla or almond essence for a flavour twist or 1 shot of espresso to enhance the chocolate

To make it Vegan

A good quality dark chocolate will only have pure ingredients with no additives or traces of milk products. Green & Black's is perhaps the most well known, but there are other brands fairly traded and certainly suitable. Don't use the eggs, bien sûr, and substitute the crème fraîche with double the quantity of a good quality soy yogurt.

variations

Dark chocolate has a high magnesium content & a deficiency of it exacerbates PMT. Perhaps this explains cravings for chocolate amongst menstruating women? It's a good excuse anyway!

Hazel ~ ancient Celtic tree of knowledge

Very good for wisdom, weaving, walking & warm winter cakes

Long thought of as a symbol of wisdom & learning, the Hazel represents potential & embodied energy. Nuts are seen as a concentration of wisdom ~ something highly nutritious, yet compact. In a nutshell ~ something sweet to the taste, just as knowledge is sweet.

Ingredients

175g butter

200g brown sugar

50ml runny honey

50ml maple syrup

3 free range eggs

250g self raising flour

2 tea spoons baking powder

1 tea spoon cinnamon

2 tea spoons cayenne pepper (I said it was warming!)

250g butter nut squash, skin removed & grated

1 apple, cored & grated

zest & juice of 1 orange

50g hazelnuts, roasted & chopped

icing sugar to decorate

In the summer, substitute the squash with it's cousin the courgette

Warming Winter Cake
with butter nut squash & hazelnuts

1 Heat the oven to 18C / gas 4. Grease a 30cm loose bottomed cake tin.

2 Melt the butter, sugar, syrup and honey in a saucepan, then leave to cool.

3 Roast the hazelnuts for 5 minutes, then chop coarsely when cool.

4 Sift the flour, baking powder and spices together. Beat the eggs and whisk into the butter mixture, then stir in the flour mixture, grated squash, apple, orange zest & juice, and finally the chopped hazelnuts.

5 Pour into the prepared cake tin and bake for 35 to 40 minutes or until cooked. Allow to cool. Dust with icing sugar when ready to serve.

did you know ...

Butter nut squash was such an important part of the diet of Native American Indians that they buried it along with the dead to provide nourishment on their final journey ... but don't just save it for the dead, use it for the Living ~ bake in the oven until tender ~ cut into chunks for steaming, sautéing or roasting then fold into pasta or risotto ~ mash or puree ~ add it to soups & stews.

Melt in your mouth nutty butter Marvel

It's the tastiest of winter squashes and sweet & succulent enough to deserve the name "butternut". It's a relative of the melon & cucumber, and its summer cousin is the courgette. It's an extremely healthy food to include in your diet since it's packed with lots of carotenes, vitamins C, A, B1, B6, magnesium, potassium, Omega-3 fatty acids, copper, and zinc. It's high in fibre, low in fat and considered one of the most heart-friendly and all-round nourishing foods to eat.

Super cinnamon

Drink it! Eat it! Apply it!
~ it's good for you

Considered one of the oldest spices, cinnamon is from the bark of a small tree grown in India, Sri Lanka, Indonesia, Brazil, Vietnam and Egypt.

There are two types ~ Ceylon (also known as true) cinnamon and Cassia, the more common variety.

It's very high in antioxidants & rich in natural compounds. Cinnamon is a great source of manganese, fibre, iron & calcium and for centuries has been used for its numerous health benefits ~ from the common cold to diabetes type 2, with arthritis, toothache & balding in between.

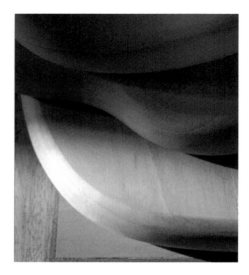

Stylish & sustainable

~ souvenirs by Sean

Beech is best when it comes to chopping boards ~ the perfect partner to the chic chef

46

Pecan & Cinnamon Cake

Vegan cakes & desserts don't have to be so tricky once you know the following egg substitutes ~ 1 egg = 1 well mashed banana or 3 table spoons apple sauce or 62.5ml (2 fl oz) blended silken tofu. Commercial egg substitute is also available. Note that when either banana or apple sauce is used, it will impart its fruity flavour to the overall taste

1 Heat the oven to 180C / gas 4. Lightly grease & line a cake tin and set aside.

2 Beat the vegan margarine with the sugar until light & fluffy, then add the sour 'cream', oil, milk and vanilla.

3 Sift together the dry ingredients (except the pecans). Add to the butter mixture, combine until smooth and creamy. Stir in the chopped pecans.

4 Pour evenly into the cake tin. Bake for 30-35 minutes, or until cooked.

What do Vegans look like?

There is an artisanal craft gallery & café run by Mary & Joff Williams which we always recommend to our guests. The drive to it is through spectacular and typical French countryside, it's veggie & vegan friendly and another place to pick up great souvenirs (as well as here). When Robert, the vegan raw foody stayed with us, I called Mary in advance to book him in & chat about his (other!) dietary requirements. Our regular UTLT table was prepared, Mary was all set, but one of her assistants had never seen a vegan before so instead of being her usual helpful self, she found any excuse to run into the restaurant to take a peep at the *vegan*. And guess what? She thought 'they' looked much healthier than the rest of us! Thanks Robert for taking your pointy ears off especially for the occasion!

Vegan

Ingredients

50g vegan margarine

210g sugar

180ml sour 'cream'

90ml oil

120ml soy milk

1 tea spoon vanilla extract

340g plain flour

1 tea spoon baking powder

½ tea spoon baking soda

½ tea spoon salt

1 tsp ground cinnamon

150g pecans, chopped (reserve a few whole ones for decoration)

For the Sour 'Cream', blend the following in a food processor until smooth and creamy

300g soft (silken) tofu, 1 tbsp oil, 1 tbsp lemon juice, 2 tsps apple cider vinegar, 1 tsp sugar, 1 tbsp soy sauce

Lightning Source UK Ltd.
Milton Keynes UK
259610UK00002B/5